EGYPT

EGYPT

Photography by Kazuyoshi Nomachi
Text by Robert Morkot

HARRAP COLUMBUS

Published by Harrap Limited,
19-23 Ludgate Hill, London EC4M 7PD
and The Guidebook Company Limited,
The Penthouse, 20 Hollywood Road, Central,
Hong Kong

Text and captions by Robert Morkot

Photography by Kazuyoshi Nomachi. Additional photographs by Lorenzo Martinengo (23, 42—43, 66, 67, 69).

Designed by Joan Law Design & Photography
Colour separations by Rainbow Graphic Arts Co., Ltd.
Jacket colour separations by Sakai Lithocolour
Printed in Hong Kong

ISBN: 0-7471-0114-0

Title spread
Although the deserts covering much of Egypt have long been regarded as hostile places by the valley dwellers, they were crossed by the caravan routes to the south and west into Africa, routes which became much easier to traverse when the camel was introduced.

Right
Luxor, the tomb of the Vizier Ramose (ca. 1360 BC). Adorned in his festival clothes, a relative of the vizier shares in the eternal banquet. The unpainted relief decoration in the tomb of Ramose is one of the finest monuments surviving from the reign of Amenhotep III (ca. 1386-1349 BC), when Egypt was at the pinnacle of her power and magnificence.

Pages 6-7
Cemeteries ancient and modern at Giza. The Great Pyramid of Cheops (centre) and the Pyramid of Chephren (left) dominate the tombs of family members and courtiers, as well as the modern Muslim cemetery (foreground). The Sphinx and the Valley Temple stand at the bottom of the causeway along which the king's mummified body was carried to his burial.

Pages 8-9
Abu Simbel, the Sanctuary of the Great Temple. Carved from the rock, the four gods of the temple await their offerings: (left to right) Ptah, the lord of Memphis; Amun-Re of Thebes with his high feathered crown; Ramesses II himself and the hawk-headed sun god Re-Harakhty. The temple was designed so that on certain days of the year the figures of Amun-Re and the king would be lit by the rays of the rising sun.

Pages 10-11
Near El-Minya, Middle Egypt. Early morning mist shrouds farmers going to work in the rich agricultural land of Middle Egypt.

Pages 12-13
Cairo. Traffic congestion is a familiar sight as vehicles converge to cross from the west bank, over the island (Gezira), to the city centre on the east bank.

Mediterranean Sea
Alexandria
Port- Said
Ismailiya
Cairo
Giza
Suez
Qattâra Depression
Sinai
El Faiyum
Beni Suef
El Minya
Beni Hasan
EASTERN DESERT
Asyut
WESTERN DESERT
Farafra Oasis
Sohag
Qena
Dendara
Karnak
Luxor
Red Sea
Dakhla Oasis
Kharaga Oasis
Isna
Idfu
Kom Ombo
Aswan
Lake Nasser
EGYPT
Abu Simbel
River Nile
SUDAN

INTRODUCTION

EGYPT presents the visitor with many striking contrasts, particularly in its landscape and in the ancient, Christian and Islamic elements of its heritage. Signs of Westernization and tradition are sometimes found in startlingly incongruous juxtaposition, but more usually the new is adapted to blend harmoniously with the old. The country itself is united by the great river which flows down its entire length, and which is indeed the creator of the country.

Without the Nile Egypt would not exist. Along its banks the majority of the people live and cultivate the land as their ancestors have done for thousands of years. This narrow, fertile valley is flanked by the desert — a desert which is always threatening to take over the cultivation. Today controlled by dams and barrages, the Nile no longer floods the country every year. The building of the High Dam at Aswan flooded the whole of the Nile valley between Aswan and the frontier with Sudan, creating Lake Nasser. Preserved from the threat of devastating floods, Egypt is now protected from the dangers of famine by the regulation of the water.

The two branches of the Nile, one rising in the highlands of Ethiopia, the other in Lake Victoria, unite at Khartoum. Flowing north through the deserts of Nubia and punctuated by the rocky Cataracts, the river enters Egypt at the Second Cataract. Aswan itself stands on the First Cataract, the final great band of granite to break the river's northward course. The Cataract created many rapids and islands which, until the end of the last century, made travel dangerous.

Egypt has a landscape which is surprisingly varied, but all of the terrain derives from a combination of water and sky, cultivation and desert. North of Aswan the river flows on without further interruptions to navigation through the orange sandstone hills of Nubia, where the cultivation in many places is confined to a narrow strip by the water's edge. The forked trunk of the *dom*-palm and the misty foliage of the tamarisk relieve the barrenness. After the fertile open plain at Kom Ombo the sandstone hills close in, forcing the river through the gorge of Silsila before giving way to the limestone cliffs which will form the valley as far as the Delta. Broad but shallow, the river meanders between these cliffs, sometimes in the centre of the valley, sometimes hugging the cliff close to one side. Throughout Upper and Middle Egypt the floodplain is broad, and the cultivation rich: there are fields of wheat and sugar cane, and groves of palm trees everywhere. In the Faiyum the lushness increases. Roads run between orchards which are enclosed by high mud-brick walls crowned with dried palm fronds. Within the orchards, a dappled light filters through the palm trees; shady walkways are canopied with vines and roses, and flanked by orange and lemon trees, mango and banana. The quiet is disturbed only by the cooing of turtle doves and pigeons, perhaps the iridescent green flash of a bee-eater, or the call of the hoopoe.

All cultivation stops as one approaches the shores of the eerie Lake Qarun. Flat and salty, the narrow lake is long from east to west, its far shore an unbroken band of desert. North of Cairo the Delta opens out, its roads lined with tamarisk and eucalyptus trees which meet overhead. Its open fields with scattered palm trees and, in the distance, denser groves, have a breadth not found elsewhere in Egypt.

The village houses, in many places still built from sun-dried mud brick, belong to the landscape, appearing to have grown out of the ground itself. Strung out along the edge of the irrigation canals, or built close together in narrow, twisting streets, the villages have a quiet dignity.

Cairo, with its tower blocks, its flyovers and ceaseless traffic, is like modern cities the world over. But amongst all this rush and bustle the life of the village has been transferred to the city in the street-side cafés and markets, and in the presence of goats weaving their way through the traffic.

Head of Ramesses II at Luxor Temple.

Broken head from statue of Ramesses II, Luxor Temple.

The mighty monuments of the pharaohs and of the Greeks and Romans, the magnificent mosques, the Coptic monasteries — both the ones which lie in ruins and those still thriving — all reflect the many stages of Egypt's rich past. Yet, amidst the signs of change, Egypt continues to exude a strong sense of unchangeability. There is much in the life of the countryside which also evokes the past: the daily and seasonal cycles of farming life seem in many ways to be little different from the scenes depicted on the tombs of three or four thousand years ago. The *shaduf* and the *saqia* wheel are still used to lift water from the river to the canals, and from the canals to the fields. The simple plough drawn by oxen or camels, the winnowing of wheat, and the manufacture of mud bricks and pottery, are all echoes from the past. All the same, there is much that is different. Egypt remains one of the most significant states in the Near East, and as in so many places there is conflict of 'progress' with tradition.

The many phases of Egypt's long history are seen clearly in the monuments, and much of what was depicted in ancient art can still be seen today. The landscape, however, has been much altered. The papyrus swamps which lined the river banks and covered whole areas of the Delta have disappeared. The papyrus itself no longer grows wild in Egypt. Along with the swamps, wildlife has been driven farther south into Africa. The wildlife once included the hippopotamus, a danger to people and crops, which is seen in many tomb scenes being hunted with harpoons. To the ancient Egyptians it was also a symbol of fertility, and the pregnant hippopotamus goddess was believed to protect women in childbirth. The crocodile, another river creature that is both feared and revered, was patron god of the Faiyum region. By the mid-19th century the crocodile had been hunted out of Egypt, and could not be found north of the Second Cataract. The desert wildlife has also been pushed further south by the encroachment of man and the desiccation of the region.

Ostriches, antelopes and lions were hunted here in ancient times, but they must all now be sought in the savannas of the Sudan and East Africa. It is not only the wildlife that has changed. Neither the camel, the immediate image of a desert country, nor the water buffalo, always to be seen basking in the canals or river, can be found in ancient art. Both were relatively late introductions to Egypt, the camel by the Persians in the fifth century BC, and the water buffalo by the Mamelukes. Over the centuries new fruits and crops have been introduced for food, or, as with cotton, for trade. In the 19th century many tropical trees and plants were brought into Egypt, which have altered its appearance further. The eucalyptus trees which line the roads, and the bougainvillaea which flourishes in Aswan, have now become part of the landscape.

Egypt's position in the eastern Mediterranean has assured it an important political role throughout history. Even when the country itself was difficult for Europeans to visit, its ancient power and splendour were an irresistible lure to adventurous travellers.

Long before the science of Egyptology developed there was much to focus the Western mind upon the country. Egypt figures in many of the major episodes of the Biblical narrative. The story of Joseph; Moses and the Exodus; the campaigns of Shishak, king of Egypt, against Jerusalem all created images of Egypt as a great power, often in opposition to the Jews. Yet, according to the account in the New Testament, with the flight of the Holy Family into Egypt the country became a haven from the despotism of Herod. Indeed, Christianity flourished in Egypt, and monasticism was developed there. The Saints and the hermits who retired to the desert to lead a life of contemplation, often living in ancient tombs, were deeply revered. St Mark, who took Christianity to Egypt; St Anthony; St Catherine of Alexandria; and St Athanasius are honoured by the churches of the East and West today. During the Middle Ages Egypt and Sinai were included in the pilgrim route to the Holy Land. On the island of Roda, near Cairo, pilgrims were shown the place where Moses was found by the daughter of Pharaoh. The tree where the Holy Family rested on the flight into Egypt flourished at Heliopolis into the 19th century. This Biblical background continued to be influential and was one of the major inspirations for early archaeological work in the country.

The civilization of western Europe owed much to its classical inheritance, which was continually being revived during the Middle Ages and the Renaissance. In the preserved books of Greek and Roman authors there was a great deal of information on Egypt, which confirmed and added to the importance accorded to the country in the Biblical traditions. Albeit garbled and, when detailed, confined to the latest periods of Egypt's ancient history, these works were important at a time when Egypt was part of the Turkish Empire and difficult to visit beyond Cairo.

The Greeks were awed by the antiquity of Egypt, so much so that they regarded it as the founder of religious ceremonies, and its culture was a great influence upon their own politics, art and religion. Herodotos visited Egypt in the middle of the fifth century BC and wrote extensively, if not always accurately, about the country, its people and its monuments. The scale of these massive structures was as staggering to visitors then as it is to those of today. Herodotos and others wrote in detail about the 'Labyrinth', a vast temple attached to the pyramid of King Amenemhat III (1842-1797 BC), which stood at the entrance to the Faiyum. Considered to be more impressive than the pyramids of Giza, the temple apparently had 3,000 rooms and many twisting passages. Today nothing survives of this marvel but a few broken columns.

The time-scale of ancient Egypt is for many people difficult to comprehend. When Herodotos visited Egypt, at a time when Greek civilization flourished, Egypt's days of greatest glory were already past. Such a time-scale can only be grasped when we remember that Cleopatra stands closer in time to us than she did to the builders of the pyramids.

With the invasion of Egypt by Alexander the Great in 332 BC, Egypt entered a period of Greek domination. After Alexander's death in 323 BC, Egypt was seized by the general Ptolemy, who captured Alexander's body and took it for burial in Alexandria. Under Ptolemy's successors Egypt continued to be the leading cultural and political power in the eastern Mediterranean. The Library and Museum of Alexandria were renowned for being centres of scholarship, and the city itself for its beauty and magnificence. The Lighthouse of Alexandria, the Pharos, was regarded as one of the Seven Wonders of the World.

Eventually, however, the descendants of Ptolemy began to fight amongst themselves. The brother-sister marriages, alliances, murders and treacheries reduced the country to a state of near civil war and bankruptcy. At this point Rome, expanding its power in the eastern Mediterranean, saw the chance to exert its influence upon this most important of states. Although Rome's expansionism was successful during the reign of Ptolemy the 'Flute Player', it was his daughter who was to prove a more formidable challenge to the aggressors.

The story of Cleopatra has become one of the classics of Western literature, retold many times in drama, opera, painting and film. Even though ours is the victor's view, Cleopatra stands out as one of the great figures of history. We forget that Octavian was far from certain of defeating her, and that initially Mark Anthony was the favoured successor of Julius Caesar. The historical Cleopatra is difficult to find, so much has her legend come to dominate. Yet with her reign Egypt again shone brilliantly before being extinguished by 300 years of Roman rule.

The manner of Octavian's victory, and Egypt's importance as the 'granary of the empire', led to the country's unique position as a personal estate of the emperor. The ordinary people were reduced to a level little better than serfdom, and all privileges were in the hands of the Greek settlers and affluent Egyptians. Nevertheless, despite the

Abu Simbel; statues of Ramesses II lining the main hall.

Luxor Temple; Ramesses II

Bedouin girl with goats near Mount Sinai.

Giza; the pyramids of Mycerinus, Chephren and Cheops.

country's decline in importance, its influence in Rome was great. Egyptian religion, especially the worship of the goddess Isis, had spread throughout much of the Roman Empire even before the conquest of the country. Temples in honour of Isis and her associated gods were to be found in most major cities, and Egyptian priests officiated in her mysteries. Rome was adorned with monuments taken at the emperor's orders from the Egyptian temples. Egypt itself, especially the island of Philae, became a place of pilgrimage for the devotees of Isis. Sarapis, a god who was worshipped along with Isis, combined the Egyptian Osiris with Dionysos and Pluto. His vast temple at Alexandria housed the Library, the greatest storehouse of knowledge in the classical world. Such was its importance that it was the focus of Christian attacks in AD 391, when it, and its contents, were destroyed by fire.

Egypt's ancient monuments fascinated both the Greeks and the Romans, and they became tourist sites. Amongst the most celebrated was the singing statue at Thebes, one of the two 'Colossi of Memnon'. Split by an earthquake in 27 BC, the northernmost of the two statues of Amenhotep III (1386-1349 BC) gave out a strange musical note at dawn, a phenomenon possibly caused by the warming of the stone. The statue was believed to be of the Trojan hero, Memnon, who had been killed in battle by Achilles, and who was thought thus to greet his mother, the goddess Aurora, each morning. Graffiti and poems carved on the legs and feet of the statue record its many visitors. In the early third century, Septimius Severus had the crack repaired, rendering the image once again mute.

Few of the Roman emperors even set foot in Egypt, but one, Hadrian, did have a special devotion to the country. In AD 130, Hadrian, on a tour of the empire, arrived in Egypt. First spending two months in Alexandria, he and his entourage then sailed to Upper Egypt. However, half way to Thebes (Luxor), tragedy struck. On 30 October, Hadrian's favourite, Antinous, drowned in the Nile. Some sources say that Antinous drowned himself to thwart a prophecy which had foretold a calamity to the emperor. Hadrian was disconsolate, and declared Antinous a god. At the site of the drowning, Hadrian founded a city, Antinoe, whose ruined column-lined streets and classical theatre still stood when Napoleon's scholars visited it. Today, mountains of rubble and broken pottery are all that mark the place. Hadrian continued to Thebes, where he heard the Colossus of Memnon sing, and on his birthday he dedicated a temple to Sarapis. This small chapel still stands outside the Temple of Luxor. On his return to Rome, Hadrian had an obelisk carved in memory of Antinous, and in his villa at Tivoli he collected together many Egyptian sculptures.

As Christianity became the major religion of the empire, the temples fell into disuse, were closed, or were converted into churches. The images of the gods were defaced to render them impotent, the statues were destroyed, and the temple treasures were looted. The temple of Isis at Philae alone remained open, visited until the mid-sixth century by the Nubians, who carried the figure of the goddess south every year to bless the crops. Eventually Nubia, too, became Christian, and the island of Philae was put under the protection of the Virgin Mary and St Stephen.

In the fourth century Egypt became a province of the Eastern Roman Empire, ruled from Constantinople. However, in the seventh century a new religion arose in Arabia, and with it a change in the political complexion of the eastern Mediterranean. The Arab armies, with Islam as their creed, swiftly established an empire stretching from Iraq through Syria and Palestine, and across North Africa. Egypt under the rule of the Islamic dynasties was a centre of art and learning. Cairo was one of the greatest and most beautiful cities in the world — the city of a thousand minarets. Many of the tales in the *Thousand and One Nights* were set in Cairo, where the stories were eventually gathered together.

The crusading armies from western Europe fought in Egypt but never gained a foothold there as they did in Syria and Palestine. The sophistication and splendour of Saladin's court held them in awe, for Islamic Egypt was then at the zenith of its power. In the wake of the crusading armies were pilgrims and merchants who brought back a few small antiquities, but more importantly quantities of *mumiya* (mummies) to be sold as medicine. By the 16th century huge numbers of mummies were being exported to Europe; ground into powder, the mummy was thought to be a cure for almost every illness.

Little else was really known about the Egypt of that time beyond the fact of its being a province of the Turkish Empire. Few visitors travelled beyond Cairo, and the only monuments visited were the pyramids. Western knowledge of Egypt still relied on the Biblical and classical sources, and there was little information on the ancient monuments. This dependence is shown in the widely held belief that the Giza Pyramids were the Storehouses of Joseph. The idea was so generally accepted that the common-sense opinion of an Oxford mathematician, who disputed the belief, was not altogether welcome. He pointed out that the pyramids are almost solid with only a few small chambers inside, and that they are built of stone, not, as stated in the Bible, of brick. Furthermore, their shape meant that they were impractical as storehouses.

Greater knowledge of ancient Egypt in western Europe came with the rediscovery, during the 16th and 17th centuries, of many monuments carried off by the Roman emperors to adorn their capital. The obelisks which had decorated the temples and circuses of ancient Rome were set up once again in the square of the Papal city, now crowned with crosses. The sculptures from Hadrian's villa at Tivoli reintroduced the West to Egyptian art.

Contacts increased in the 18th century, and with an increase in trade, more small antiquities reached Europe. Although some books began to appear with illustrations of the monuments in the southern part of the country, Egypt was still infrequently visited. All this changed in 1798 when the ambitions of France and Britain clashed in the eastern Mediterranean. Napoleon invaded Egypt, and Britain, in order to prevent French domination of the route to India, followed. Alongside Napoleon's military expedition came a large group of scholars who travelled throughout the whole country recording monuments and collecting objects. This was the turning point in the West's knowledge of Egypt and its cultures, a knowledge increased over the past hundred years by the efforts of archaeology.

The decipherment of hieroglyphics brought the names of Ramesses II, Amenhotep III and the other great builders of ancient Egypt to the attention of the world. The early 19th century saw the removal of large numbers of statues and other objects to the museums of western Europe. Expeditions from the scientific academies of France, Italy and Germany recorded the monuments in great detail. Knowledge rapidly increased. In the second half of the century more scientific methods of archaeology were developed. This led to a shift of interest and, instead of concentrating on the massive monuments of stone, Egyptian archaeology concerned itself with small objects, the things of everyday life. Egypt has also seen some of the most spectacular of archaeological discoveries. The Tomb of Tutankhamun (1334-1325 BC), uncovered in 1922, has a perennial fascination, and has created its own mythology — the 'Curse of the Pharaohs'. The huge quantity of gold buried with this king lures crowds to Cairo Museum every year. The massive gold coffin, the superb death mask, the elaborate jewellery of gold and precious stones, the strange gilt statue of the funerary deities, hold visitors spellbound. If this is what was buried with a young king who reigned barely ten years, and whose name was hardly known from the monuments, what treasures must have been buried with Ramesses II?

Sinai.

Qena; A Coptic priest reads the Sunday service.

In many ways village life has changed little since ancient times. The winnowing of wheat (top) can be seen in tomb paintings 3,000 years old.

Right
Village girl, Beni Hasan

Of all the pharaohs it is Ramesses II (1279-1212 BC) whose name is most often seen carved in massive hieroglyphs almost everywhere in Egypt. In the 1960s removal of his temples at Abu Simbel to save them from the waters of Lake Nasser, captured the public imagination, and today plane loads of visitors fly everyday from Aswan over the lake to visit them. Few places in Egypt are more striking. The vast and confusing remains of Karnak, the Valley of the Kings with its mysterious paintings of the underworld, and the delicate temples of Philae, all impress in their own way, but Abu Simbel is a work of unparalleled grandeur. Its façade, carved from the cliff face, is dominated by four seated statues of the king each 22 metres (72 feet) high. Standing on either side of the king and reaching just to his knees are figures of his mother and wives, with smaller statues of some of his children. The temple's halls are cut deep into the rock. The first, its ceiling supported by square columns with massive statues of the king lining the aisle, is decorated with scenes of the king's battle with the Hittites at Kadesh in north Syria. Smaller rooms lead to the holy of holies where four great statues of the temple's deities await their offerings. Egypt's revered gods — Ptah, the Lord of Memphis, the ancient capital city near present-day Cairo; Amun-Re, the chief god of Thebes (Luxor), wearing a tall feather headdress; and Re-Harakhty, the hawk-headed sun god — flank the most important god of all, Ramesses II himself. On two days of the year the rays of the morning sun strike straight down the temple's axis to illuminate the figure of Egypt's most famous god-king.

Here at Abu Simbel the ancient and modern combine: the amazing engineering skill of the ancient Egyptians is paralleled by the equally staggering modern feat of raising the temple from the valley to its new site. The statues, which once watched the course of the Nile, now stare out over the waters of Lake Nasser.

Abu Simbel. Ramesses II's temple is one of the most striking of all Egypt's monuments. Carved from the cliff face, four seated figures of the king, accompanied by his wife and children, dominate the entrance (left). The roof of the main hall is supported by pillars with statues of the king carrying the crook and flail, symbols of the royal office (above). The protective wings of the vulture goddess spread across the painted ceiling.

Right
Seated statue of Ramesses II at Abu Simbel, the king's wife and mother at either side, and his daughter between his legs.

Preceding page
Kom Ombo. Ptolemy VII (145-116 BC) pulls himself through the marsh towards the fertility god, Min, in this relief in the temple of Kom Ombo. Above, the king makes offerings to one of the temple's chief deities, the crocodile-headed Sobek. Beneath, the king and his sister-wife, Cleopatra II, are followed by a procession of Nile gods bringing the produce of the districts of Egypt.

At Aswan, boats sail around the islands of the Cataract. The largest island, Elephantine (on the left), may have received its name because the massive granite boulders look like elephants bathing in the river.

Temple of Isis at Philae (2nd — 1st centuries BC), Aswan. Situated on a small island in the heart of the Cataract, Philae was known to visitors in the 19th century as the Pearl of the Nile. The temple has now been rebuilt on a higher island to save it from the waters of the reservoir. Large figures of the goddess Isis and her son, the hawk-headed Horus, flank the doorway of one of the most charming temples in Egypt. The two niches held flag poles which rose above the temple roof.

The Temple of Luxor. Connected with the temples at Karnak by a sphinx-lined road 3 kilometres (1.9 miles) long, Luxor Temple was visited by the statues of Amun, his wife and son, in a great annual festival. The courtyard of the temple is lined with statues of Ramesses II, their heads now lying at their feet (above). Ramesses II, followed by his chief wife, Nefertari, superintends the raising of the May-pole for the fertility god, Min-Amun. Beneath, a procession of some of the king's sons bring offerings of flowers (right).

The temple of Amun at Karnak, Luxor. The colossal floodlit statue is of Ramesses II. With the crook and flail crossed on his chest, he stands stiffly before the temple's gateway. His daughter stands on his feet, but even so scarcely reaches his knees.

Above
The head of Ramesses II, Western Thebes

The Colossi of Memnon at Luxor, West Bank. Believed by the Greeks to represent the hero Memnon, slain at Troy by Achilles, these two colossi stood at the entrance of the now destroyed temple of Amenhotep III (1366-1349 BC). The northern (right-hand) statue gave out a musical note with the rising of the sun. The sound was believed to be the cry of the dead hero to his mother, the goddess of the dawn.

Left
The Temple of Hatshepsut at Deir el-Bahari (1498-1483 BC), Luxor, West Bank. In one of the most spectacular of settings, the Temple of Hatshepsut rises up from elegant terraces. Behind the cliffs lies the Valley of the Kings. Now in the stark desert, the temple once had gardens, and groves of trees were planted in front of it.

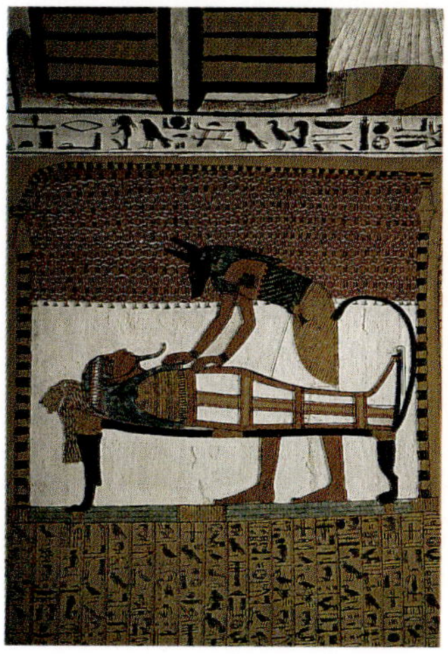

Luxor, West Bank, the tombs of the Nobles. The nobles' tombs are decorated with elegant paintings to continue the life of this world into eternity. In the tomb of Sennefer, the Mayor of Thebes (top), which is dated to ca. 1450 BC, the ceiling is painted with colourful geometric designs, whilst the scenes on the walls show Sennefer receiving food and drink from his wife. Musicians in the tomb of Nakht (above right) entertain the tomb owner with harp, lute and double-flute. The body of Sennedjem, an overseer of workmen, lies on a lion-shaped bed whilst Anubis, the jackal-headed inventor of mummification, prepared him for the afterlife (above left).

Above
The painted houses in Farafra Oasis indicate that the owner has been on the pilgrimage to Mecca.

Right
Near Kharga Oasis, Western Desert. Several large oases lie in the hostile desert, and have since ancient times been occupied by both Egyptians and Bedouin.

Left
Wearing the traditional black and coloured robes of the Bahriya Oasis, this woman has tattooed forehead and chin. The nose ring, worn by women in the Faiyum and the oases, is always of gold, never any other metal.

Above
These schoolgirls come from the Bahriya Oasis region. Bahriya is the northernmost of the oases accessible from the Nile valley. It has monuments from ancient times, as well as Roman ruins and Christian churches, so here all the aspects and periods of Egypt's history are represented.

Near Dendera. A house decorated in commemoration of the pilgrimage to Mecca.

Near El-Minya, Middle Egypt. The water buffalo is one of the commonest sights in agricultural areas, yet it is a comparatively late introduction to Egypt. Brought from India during the Middle Ages, it has ousted the many kinds of cattle shown in ancient art.

The quietness of work in the fields contrasts with the bustle of the markets in Middle Egypt. Camels are loaded up with the wheat harvest. The horse-drawn carriage, the gharry, is one of the favourite means of transport in smaller towns, where people come from outlying villages to sell their produce.

Right
Near Qena: Some 5-10% of the population remain Christian, many living in the region south of El-Minya. Most are adherents of the Coptic Church, the most ancient of the Christian traditions, with its own Pope. The Patriarchy of Alexander is said to have been founded by St Mark, whose body, buried in Alexandria, was later stolen by the Venetians.

Left
The river is the supplier of all water.

The eroded landscape (left) does not seem like the typical desert of fine sand and windswept dunes. Nomads use richly woven cloth as part of the saddling (above).

Farafra Oasis. The region around this oasis is marked by extraordinary hillocks of denuded chalk.

Kharga Oasis. The land is rich, but the desert is always threateningly close by.

Bahriya Oasis. Far from the Nile, the oases are situated in depressions in the desert, their water appearing as springs, or in small lakes.

Although modern methods of agriculture are found in many places, more traditional technology can still be seen. The simple plough is of a type used since the beginning of Egyptian history (left).

A quicker and more efficient method of raising water than the shaduf, *the* saqiya *(top) was introduced into Egypt in the first century BC. A wheel, turned by an ox or donkey, rotates a second wheel which has water pots attached. Today the* saqiya *is often driven by motor.*

The shaduf *(right and opposite) is the simplest method of raising water from the river to the canals, or onto the fields. Consisting of a bucket on a long weighted pole, this device can be seen in tomb paintings of 3,000 years ago.*

Near Qena. In a country with virtually no rainfall, houses have traditionally been made from unfired mud brick. The simplicity of the architecture, and the colour and texture of the material, give such buildings a dignity lacking in burnt red brick and concrete. The water jars built into the walls are decorative, but also provide insulation (above).

Nile mud has always had many uses: for fertilising the land, for building, and for the pottery utensils of daily life (opposite).

The water of the Nile gives life to Egypt. Now controlled by the Aswan Dam, the river no longer floods every year. Today, with the building of roads southwards from Cairo, the river is used less for transport. In ancient times it was the main highway for the transport of goods and armies, pilgrimages, and where the festivals of the gods, as well as the business of the officials, were conducted.

Giza, the Great Pyramid. Built for Khufu (Cheops, ca 2589-2566 BC) of the fourth dynasty, the Great Pyramid has since ancient times been acknowledged as one of the wonders of the world. Its builder called it 'the pyramid which is the place of the sunrise and the sunset'; its shape may represent the rays of the sun by which the dead king climbed to heaven.

Giza, the Great Pyramid. It no longer has its smooth outer casing blocks, which were pillaged for the building of mediaeval Cairo. This man-made mountain contains about 2,352,000 cubic metres (3,076,400 cubic yards) of stone, the largest weighing 15 tons. It has been estimated that if all of the blocks were sawn into cubes 30 centimetres (one foot) in each dimension, then placed side by side, they would cover a distance equal to two-thirds of the circumference of the world at the equator. The exact method of its construction, however, remains uncertain.

Giza, the Pyramid of Chephren (ca. 2258-2532 BC). Slightly smaller than the Great Pyramid, the Pyramid of Chephren stands on a low hill, and thereby dominates its larger neighbour. The upper part still carries its smooth limestone casing blocks, which were originally glistening white but are now weathered.

Following page
Once approached by a long, shady, tree-lined road, the Giza Pyramids now look out over the urban sprawl of modern Cairo which has spread out to the foot of the pyramids. The skyline, dominated by the tower blocks of the major hotels, and the radio and post office towers, is like that of many modern cities the world over.

SIAG

2912

Egypt remains a predominantly Muslim country. The Friday noon prayer, the most important of the week, halts traffic in Cairo city centre (opposite). A shop window displays the traditional headcloths of orthodox Muslim women (above middle), whilst Ramesses II stands serenely amidst the tower blocks, flyovers and hoardings of the modern city (above).

Cairo's main roads know no rush-hour — from early morning to late evening they are blocked with traffic (right).

A drink seller in the street, Cairo. The glasses are carried in the metal container at his waist, while the large bottle contains one of the traditional liquors, karkade, *made from the flowers of the hibiscus flower, or the bitter-sweet* tamarindi. *The brass hand-amulet is there to ward off the evil eye.*

In Cairo, the street-side cafés are a place to meet and talk, and drink mint tea. Gambling is forbidden by Islamic law, but card games and backgammon are popular café pastimes.

The Egyptian Museum, Cairo. One of the greatest treasure houses in the world, the Cairo Museum contains hundreds of important works of art. But the chief attraction is always the burial goods of Tutankhamun. The excitement of the tomb's discovery, its wealth, and the youth of the king, exert a perennial fascination.

A supreme example of Egyptian goldwork, the mask of Tutankhamun is an idealized portrait of the young king. In this perfected state he was to live for eternity. Gold was the flesh of the gods, so it was fitting that a dead king should be encased in a golden coffin.

Among the treasures of the Egyptian Museum, Cairo, is this life-size statue of Tutankhamun, one of a pair which guarded the entrance to the burial chamber. The black indicates the king's rebirth.

Gilt wooden statue of Tutankhamun, wearing the white crown of Upper Egypt with the protective serpent, at the Egyptian Museum, Cairo (opposite).

The minarets of the Mosque of al-Rifa'i, Cairo (opposite). Built opposite one of Cairo's noblest mosques, that of Sultan Hassan, al-Rifa'i has deceived many tourists into thinking it is of the same date (1356). In fact it is a splendid example of the Mameluke revival. It was begun in 1869 for the Princess Khushyar, mother of the Khedive Ismail (reigned 1863-79), but not completed until 1912. Modelled upon the finest mediaeval Cairene mosques, it contains burials of some of the Egyptian royal family, and the last Shah of Iran.

The Citadel, Cairo (above). The mighty fortress was built by Saladin on a hill overlooking Cairo. The Alabaster Mosque was built by Mohammed Ali, who ruled Egypt from 1805 to 1848. Its burnished domes now dominate the Cairo skyline. In design it is Turkish, with pencil minarets, and a departure in style from the traditional Egyptian types of the al-Rifa'i.

Following page
Cairo by night seen from the east bank, looking south and west. The skyline of modern Cairo conceals the village life which has been brought there and continues amongst the hotels and roadways.

Alexandria. For three centuries from the time of Alexander the Great to the death of Cleopatra (30 BC), Alexandria was the mistress of the Mediterranean, the glittering capital city of Ptolemaic Egypt. Its fortunes were revived when it became a trading city in the 19th century.

Alexandrian society, ancient and modern, has been immortalized in the works of C.P.Cavafy, E.M.Forster, Lawrence Durrell and Naguib Mahfouz. Today little remains of its ancient glory and more recent romance.

The Suez Canal. A source of wealth but also of conflict, de Lesseps' canal was built at the height of European influence in Egypt and at the encouragement of the Khedive Ismail, then seized back when Egypt asserted her independence. Its opening, for which Verdi composed his Egyptian opera, Aida, *was attended by the French Empress Eugenie. Later, Ismail's extravagance forced him to sell his shares in the canal. They were snapped up by Disraeli for the British government, which thereby acquired a 44% control.*

Sinai. In ancient times a place of mining expeditions, it later became a destination of pilgrimages. The Monastery of St Catherine (opposite) is one of the oldest and most revered in Christendom. Near the place where Moses received the Ten Commandments, and the site of the Burning Bush, this is a holy place for Jews, Christians and Muslims.

Monastery of St Catherine, Sinai. As so often in Egypt the art of one religion is blended with that of others. Here the altar and icons reflect the Byzantine traditions, but the tiles are Islamic work.

Right
Monastery of St Catherine: a fine Byzantine mosaic depicting the Virgin and Child.

Following page
Going home at the end of the day.

ΜΡ